MILES PRESS

Indiana University South Bend Department of English

ULTRA-CABIN

42 Miles Press
Editor, David Dodd Lee
Copyright© 2016 Kimberly Lambright. All rights reserved.
ISBN: 978-0-9830747-7-9 (pbk. alk. paper)

For permission, required to reprint or broadcast more than several lines, write to:
42 Miles Press, Department of English, Indiana University South Bend
1700 Mishawaka Avenue, South Bend, IN 46615

www.42milespress.com

Art Direction: Nicholas Kuder, Design: Michaela Penberthy, Production: Paul Sizer
The Design Center, Frostic School Of Art, Western Michigan University.
Printing: McNaughton & Gunn, Inc.

ULTRA-CABIN

POEMS
BY
KIMBERLY
LAMBRIGHT

CONTENTS

II.

III.

All this and not ordinary, not unordered in not resembling.
The difference is spreading.

—Gertrude Stein

A LIMIT SITUATION

Punch him in the top of the head.
Like a bop?

I don't mind
the calculation or the law
stacked at your dresser or even

the other wife, in the other state, smoking cigarettes.

Like a standardized test, I'm made
to instigate guessing. *Guessing*

is the only way to take advantage of your partial knowledge.

Upon a close reading. Oven-baked wheat.
Or the giant expression on my face.

To say a giant expression isn't to tell you what
but how much and this is how you talk

to me, in levels, in saying, if it was this
it would be this much.

As if I am driven by amount. I am
driven by amount.

I.

(RE)LENT

He needed that lack
of spin, the holy spring

Hers was a rust
rainbow, pinked-out edges

It's my place not yours
to say what in my hands

is failing

MARGAUX

Liquid elocution, what a fox.
The pressing and the majestic
indent – I colored on the line,
along the ridge my sister came back,
she was a refracting jewel,
predicting my mood of wool, my mulled wood.
She took my hand but it was
a lie: I am the hungry one,
never passive, giving passage, only
pressure. The flannel idea
brought comfort and the window
fell open to a gray pastoral.

The type of baking that
renders emergency dull.

NIGHT TASKS

All evening
you quote Foucault.
The tea burns,

my doll-self
traveling the length
of your neo-thighs.

Politics,
the way you interpret
the dark world happening to you.

I prefer god-smacking
you while my friend
is there, biting her lip.

The headache in your knee,
the dull look away.

Tell me what
makes the warlords cum,
bag up that continental.

I'm sailing out
here.
Crying out
here.
Dying out.

AWAITING SUMMER

Begin in absolute peeling. Shrill
midnight mercy
like no electricity, supine aside
the sliding door to
all that green sky.

Begin the turn into
the kind center of terror,
the "don't hassle me"
the "come here."

Begin just this.
Just this notice.
The no-place, the no
thing. I have an aqua eyeball
hungering out to you.

BOLD, THE FAVORS

Come by, this wind. Tangential steps, light tick
and old pain. The sorrow in the tarot cards

placed on napkins on Capitol Hill, pre-rain.
Nervous decade.

PEACH YARD

treetops of fig
overlook the orange owl and fireweed
of late capitalism

sweet collusion
cold burn

alpenglow alluvial
dirt strata amok
in wrecked light

you yank and you jam

IN RECOVERY

The bigots are talking about divine rescue
and tossing confetti,
stepping out of vanilla land.

Yawning among the UFOs,
we were young, sitting on the cooler
at that warehouse New Year's party, kissing.

Blueberry pie
somewhere in Bushwick, eroding
moon shading

your inspirational hair,
thin volume of gestalt theory
under your arm: I try to be

substance-over-style
although my soft grunge
kneads like mercy into the felted backseat.

A postmodern tabulation
in lavender-tinted aviators
I'm washed-out but I'm ultimate.

NOVEMBER

Being that
she's a planet from the green
wave affixed to this door bent
and suspending universe-wide
(the gray a line through Ecuador
or trees of similar wealth) and being
that my bony life trembles clearly

I took the call
my face shining
broken citrus leftover.
We had been in darkness.
I panned open all day, the light
settling into the room
steam aligning the wallpaper patterned
with watermelons and cherries.

RYDER

The horoscope found your hair,
twisted the long sunset in your groin.
Fortunate son, this is our year.

The blackbirds wrestle birch and snow.
Mid-sentence beside the lake
and my scream is a serving bowl. I give you
the terrible woods, animaled
and damp with fever. The elk
kicking dirt, the moon
yawning ice. My dread
of water: blue instead,
blue-rather, blue-given.

WE ARE GOING TO RETAIN THE SOFA

I am not making
the dawls. They
are dispersed and sea-form. They
foam. Again I open my arms
and nothing. Trap you. I flag
him down. The water
of man, the escape of ice
blocks up
at the door.

These poems, would they
were pre-man.
You are losing
track of me.
It hassles the birds, that wind is pre-man.
I've gone so far back
I do not remain.

GET BURN

The pine needles sorrow. Red drip sap.
Adirondack chairs flacked in all this sun. The beginning of Texas,
a blue May flower, candy necklace, the type
of lay-me-down.

Give way to the delirium shuttered in floors.
Sweet pinkish neck, length
from our hooked mouth, as one, to the ground.

SOUTHERN CALIFORNIA ANNOUNCEMENT

You're really getting places
reading that Bible over and over.

This is so current I can't think of it.
That's what I think of you:
Walk off your cherry-undertone head.

I could stay up all night watching E
profile your dumb black hair: there

was one moment in 1989
when you really surprised me.
The batter
in the kitchen circled for hours.
You move
your dull body from room
to room and this time
it's bad news.

PATAGONIA

I. Jawline

The evening's landfall blue,
the Andes unbuckling.
I tended to be rigid within the basalt,
the burnout. *No,* I don't want to party,
take your white eyes to the broken sea.

My thinking follows a line,
logocentric beneath your situation.

II. Floral Parka

The hikers traveled widely, speed and lucking.
The heritage form, I remained
cold at the medieval furnace,
wanting to establish an archive
of elected hummingbirds, structuralism,
of buttons sewn and replete.

III. Green-white

It blows so hard when you're alone.
You can hear the blown worlds
wayfaring by you. I stuck three pancakes
in your hand and begged, you palmed
my shoulders to the canyon wall.

Like everyone I spent the first half
of my life in bed with the overlord.

IV. Trill

My slag. Drawn to the orographic
winter within. My face is modern.
I'm trying to say everything in the mint
wash of my modern face.

FIRM

Launder this pale ledge,
triple brain on triple power,
log up and surf up –
I made a brain cake upon
a winter landscape. Those boys
at the Brooklyn bar are
tripping out and naming babies
like drinks: Pollyanna Rocker,
Icelandic Bitterwood.
I keep going to this fabric class called Gentle.

AIM

You're doing the blue things in far
fields. Off in that potato
land my mind folded like a daughter,
the rich glance of the year.
When we last spoke, you didn't
need a black-haired girl screaming
love you so much into the
remarkable spaces of your jacket.
Trying to cry. Crying too. Trying
for you to bend and spend.
I said lateral and I meant revert.
You said love and you meant flattery.
That girl is skating again, who skates?
Today the moon wore yellow and wrote an ode,
it was full of laziness. It was the type of ode
you say without conviction,
as if you'd earned a black flower.

ANOMIE

I leash my blue to the lit
hallway trilled
by sisters bent
and stammering.

And this dog barking:
his brown sag.
The pencil-eraser pink of his gums
sloshing in saliva. Not

for hunger. That's your problem.
Your bowl to dip.

IN THE FIELD OF LEMON AFTERGLOW

Your worry canoe slows to anatomy,
floral lime paper against
the breakfast table. I'm here
to tell you even honor fades
in the outback, the glim-glum,
and that you will make it. All the myth,
the decoration, the raft of your pearl,
it will bog as you remain
in the heavy sky and the bronze ring.
Your tonality lit with incubation.
I hallucinate your rib-temper, I unfurl
the ark of your blueberry forest fever dream.

II.

REDUX

The sea crows glisten and I miss you.
Off-white waves muscle and slack
at the mouth of the sky. Would you catch flight
and gnaw into my dull heart? My purchase
is imperfect but mine, an underproduction
amassing all this green foam. The ocean
lights a sadness along the wide afternoon.

MYSTERY

Rodents clog the rental car to Philadelphia where the astronaut
paints his microwave black. His mood stiffens.

I tip and set my face, clinically charmed.
Elsewhere, birds enter Walgreens and become priced objects.
Nail polish, 1-hr. photo, licorice.

I don't shop.
I wait in the car like rigor mortis.

CANNIBAL

Dark envy is not currently covered by the mood
stabilizers, nor the glass lid on Loon Lake.
It was a new family, this adultery. To come again
between them – he,
gone and abstracted: holy ghost, hunting rifle,
I was a project he didn't
fix like the beat-up truck, the gnarled deer meat.

She, pounds of jellied flesh, grotesque,
a body of fat facial features. She would not shut up.

I shut up
in a personality made
for bedroom eyes. And when they
tugged my clothes I was flush with error.
I was doughed, the over-animal,
the fat you cut off. Your husband
dug into me but I didn't want him to.
By my mute you gain your year.

BADLANDS

Tell me again about the torched canyon walls.
The soil in the valley at the ridge.
Tell me if the land is banished like you,
your *trousers*, the stoned meat in your skull.

All evening listening
& you aren't talking.
I hear only the knelt-down cavern floor
arrested in your light. Cob this errant
hollow stalk of me.

1988

He thinks I am wearing a red shirt and handing out lemonade.
Lemon Addition.
I clarify: *This is good.* Owls in his eyes,
green and rock grey. I hear a lady across the creek

wailing, whipped.
I belong in the valley of the mull.
He takes me to school,
my math book shines citrus.

I MADE UP MY MIND

In the Alaska aftermath the eyelid mountain
crests, bests

toward the ultra-cabin. I cure
the supermarket and
there is always a girl being injured perfectly,

her eyes are wolf eyes,
they will pin you down,
make you over.

THE CARDBOARD FLOOR STUCK IN SICK BROWN LIGHT

It's time to lose understatement, coy
thermodynamics. Freud wandered Vienna
with a brain full of energy

and called it the unconscious.
That's where you live, now that I don't think of you.
You lean on the pink meat of my mind.

SMOKE

The night
is nipple red

cherry tone
through the sky

We gum the chewy
bars on 4th avenue

guys from Florida
belly me

and we are
laughing lowly

We are low

TROPICAL GEMS

Open-palmed you show me your trashed knees.
Still coming down, taut sorrow spanning,

my lungs a dream box,
dumb blocks of space-pain.

I just float out. These crystal
rocks see the history, your nude
hand making treasure.

If you ever come back I will be post-swim pretty.
I will fashion the jam and special docks.

HIGH DESERT

Phenomena pheromones,
balmed herbalist
arranges the southwest apothecary

Period of synthesis,
style and thought as one,
cosmic avenue and yonder

At parties you get pulled
into the yard by drunken neverland,
distilled mineral, inland approximation

I WREAK HAVOC

Blue-ball berries, 40 dollars in the
hole. If that's not
self-perfecting
I don't know. Try-in

to hunt you down, hung
you down. Forever a daughter,
I forgive

each tiny black world.
You dick

around, you
dick.

DEAR BROOKLYN

I.

I gulf in the air and my heart's pink. The cherries
on the table beside the dresser blink.
I'm unconvinced. *Come in, it's been
a disaster without you.* I lean
to see the end
in the squares on my block. The Puerto Rican men hover
at the bodega – they see it.

II.

It is not so much
your candy streets or shorts
or the meat between your teeth.
It is my tragedy around you.
My head seeming bloody trysts.
You have hold of me,
I've set my heart in your black hair.
This year I'm ready for winter,
that TV slamming 4 stories to the ground.

TO STAY

My dove friend Amy dreams me up. Winds me up
in her static yellow house. The year we bend
into a field of glow-in-the-dark tulips, scope

a creek cardinal, heroin spoon, man
asleep on plastic and dumb falls forward. I'm learning
to hold the world in the back of my mind.

RELATION WITHIN RELATION

Which is to say the socks in the van

and the heartache and orange soda.
This is Russell's Paradox, the way

you look at me during the way
you have chosen her cheekbones

and neon pink vulva.

NOTES ON YOUR ABSENCE

This is the coral version. The premature. The amoeba.
The marine exhaustion of looking at the door. The time
our habitat was a city bus housing the jellylike mass of our drinking.
I lived in towns of vegetation and rain, so we were sad,
like open carols. We hiked strange elevations of wet soil.

NEW YEAR

No more about the body, its suitcase skin.
No more about wisdom, that shopped evening.

To have at once
the third item,
the eye
in the hull
of the ship
turning. He must
know of me,
how I case him.

NOR IS THERE ANYONE BUT US

East Village bars all lit up with punk.
The generation surges and I live after you.
By this time
you have a house and a new neurosis. A baby
named Kathy. Your wife says *Oh Oh Oh.*

I've baked a lasagna
of what could remain of our over-
spoken over-
done, over. It seethes
and steams ridiculously.

What is this distance
to the door, the word
to close the word.

The boys cooking okra
in the communal house
care more about everything.

REQUIEM

Burnt orange of the West Texas sky:
deflating raft on the pool water, white
of the yard's Mexican Blue Oak. Such a tree
gives me a smoldering feeling, here
in my flowered one-piece, not allowing
you to act awestruck when what
you are is confused.
The purple-hearted tank of wonderment gives
the most horrific dilemmas. My dark
handshake along your extreme backside.

BANQUET

junk around the drug table
dark corn

my body
remains unlaced

the juiced brain of just desire
coy burden

what have you stolen
that you can give back

CITY OF ROSES

Sinful sleep, a ghost-held
idea of cherry and white cake.
He undresses her by the television.

In the rocking she comes to it,
that oblong vision, delicate number.

POSTCARD NO. 173

Empathy is a eucalyptic kitchen.
Wax plant leaves. My voice
asleep in the porch light.

Mildew, and I drew
my breath. Fell blind. Fell
numbered into my dissertation.

Tonight, my sister palms the felted pool table,
hungry, compressed. About her

there is kicking, whole towns of ruin.

THE MOON, IT NEEDS A LIGHT

Laissez-faire is cool release, feline
attempt to hinge

lawed light. Three times
he plans their continental

field, raked and begotten. She walks

to the mailbox as if to find their children there,
pre-born and full of maple syrup.

My sick
depth of things.

THEMATIC WHITE

Subsequent sounding,
what a set up.
Evening walk in the sway,
descended alterity. The sky

itself an independent form.
They always want
sigh
consent
sigh
ceremony.

You're hardly legible in those crafty coats.
Stable without your proof,
what's available?

This grid is wholly almond.
Holy almost.

NORTH LOOP

The light tricks real shade on survival
island, realms of coconut groves
take care beside an Atlantic as unlocked
as I am becoming. My pounded wonder
topples gold. Denned in doors still, the dark
rolls over the mood water to remove love.

ALL IS FLUX

Your child is too big for a stroller, think Godzilla stuck
in my German

notebook, think ice, think
Willy Wonka,
archery camp,

think definition, think list. I'm not
terrible and

you can always not follow a rule.

If I weren't always late, where
would I be? Timely, groomed, fed, tended

in those night hours

but instead I gleam like a piece of the Brooklyn sky.
I am my own example.

PEOPLE ARE TALKING ABOUT CLINTON AGAIN

I waited in Mecca Café for you.
You were overwhelmed.
I ate a roast beef sandwich with gravy and mashed potatoes and waited.
You didn't come, you were overwhelmed.
I had a whiskey coke, talked to the waitress.
You didn't show. Who knew where you were, you
were overwhelmed.
I tapped my fingers on the table. I paid my check.
I saw a flyer about baby mice on the way out.
I walked down the street, you were overwhelmed.
Or was it baby ice?

I VERGE AND I VEER

Dear glib love, who has taken
the end of my decade(nce).

Dear entered room,
how I rescind my walk

along your sun and your shine.

The stove and (not the fridge). This notting,
this nothing. I've not
crept the slick-plaid. I (never) wanted

to be your strange condition,
your waking.
The girls, they reap (c)over.

REPOSE IS THE LEAST OF OUR PROBLEMS

We drown in the good
milk of the cat. I walk

away and away. I am away.

In the New York glare
I study concepts. I concept-glare.

A man nights off in his bedroom,

bluebird sheets, K-mart plants.
I've stopped belonging here,

I tell you, remotely,
chamber orchestra, coalescence.

Our love is that
I abandon

my esoteric armful,
restless for your suffix.

We fall hobbled,
this witchcraft month,

and the gods,
they're at cross-purposes.

PARENTAL, OR I DON'T ACTUALLY KNOW GERMAN

Friedrich Ulfers and I went to Montreal
last summer among the ducks
       and when I say weather, I mean
       vague feelings
and I nuzzled his Germanity while he
told me what it is
to represent
a representation, and for example,
we took the trees.

My need for love
is a need for guidance. For the world

to split and customize.

I kiss the uneven walls.
Drink rum
and pretend things.

But I might leave in the night,
in condition of my search.

THE LAKE MAY BECOME A HAND

Stacks of math are sunning.

The month remarks me. Glints me.
Maybe I'll give you a spot on my silver mountain.

Maybe it will be a trick, a repetition.
Because you hate to be outside.

I thought
I had you. Didn't I
have you yesterday?

INTERNALITY

I was your marbled bottom.
Round and enormous
ivory tusk.

The wafered afternoon gnaws me.
Be-sheds me
until I flake.

Against seizures, the professor
turns off the lights, says: *I can't make up my mind.*
But the city hallucinates

lit traffic at the window,
and he falls to the floor
in a thousand disco pounds.

I want my teeth in his jerking mouth
as he bangs
in the imminent flash.

TO VIE

That winter I was intoxicated
by ordinary light on
babies in afternoon sleep.
The border of glory
I'd had since youth
faded in strokes,
cards thrown
to the center of the table.
I lobbed the cream away.
Remaining, this normal jaw.

WRAP

I rest less in January, that cold cat.
Mid-winter mind. And the banks of it. Streets
go bad places, like luck:
ability to excite
anyone, slow index finger across the forehead,
that honest sentence always in my mouth.

WICKERED LIKE SPRING TO HIS CHEST

Oregon wants your lazy legs.
Your wax smile. In a weekend

of two parties, I delineate.
Step into my white dress

and claim the counter.
Counterclaim.

Which is to say: I've seduced you
to the dreamers' table,

cupcaked and iridescent.
By the punch bowl everyone

awes us,
sums us. This is probably

all right.
A reordering of the jaw.

A muscle clean
as hung case,

bog lamp.
As you touch my ear,

I hum the linoleum
of little ideas.

CLOSING THE ESTATE

You're the decade dream
I gave up. I came up
like pearl flowers from a grave.
The supermoon matters, the cosmos
matters, that
with matter.
The timelessness you invoked was less
beneficial than matter.

Cities moved for you, rearranged
their skirts under tables. Dogs
walked sheepishly to the cleaners.
To impress you. And then the turn,
a normal

morning, really: sun-lung, scratch
of shadow on the wood paneling. I was
at my grandmother's home eating cherries
alone. At once I knew I had met you
without error. The beauty left me
quickly, bird-like,
as I dwelt in the dust of the morning sun.

ACKNOWLEDGMENTS AND NOTES

Some of the poems in this book have previously appeared in these stellar publications:

(Re)lent - *Columbia Poetry Review*

Awaiting Summer, November, Wickered like Spring to His Chest - *Bone Bouquet*

Get Burn - *Sink Review*

In the Field of Lemon Afterglow, I Made Up My Mind - *The Boiler Journal*

I Wreak Havoc, Dear Brooklyn, Smoke - *Wicked Alice*

Wrap - *Poems + Prints*

"Southern California Announcement" borrows a line from Chelsey Minnis' *Bad Bad*.

"Dear Brooklyn" borrows a line from Ashley Capps' *Mistaking the Sea for Green Fields*.

"The Lake May Become a Hand" is influenced by the vernacular of Gertrude Stein.

Thanks to DDL for your confidence. And to the Inland NW Center for Writers. Love to the cities where I lived as this work formed: inconsolable Portland, hip Brooklyn, mystical Austin. And thanks of course to the unnamed special few who have given me moments of meaning.

Photo: Coren Johnston

Kimberly Lambright was born in Lewistown, Montana, in 1982 and received an MFA from Eastern Washington University and an MA in humanities from NYU. She lives in Austin, TX.

2 04